THE REALITY OF LIFE

The Reality of Life
Book of Songs

Hubert Severe

XULON PRESS

Xulon Press
2301 Lucien Way #415
Maitland, FL 32751
407.339.4217
www.xulonpress.com

© 2023 by Hubert Severe

All rights reserved solely by the author. The author guarantees all contents are original and do not infringe upon the legal rights of any other person or work. No part of this book may be reproduced in any form without the permission of the author.

Due to the changing nature of the Internet, if there are any web addresses, links, or URLs included in this manuscript, these may have been altered and may no longer be accessible. The views and opinions shared in this book belong solely to the author and do not necessarily reflect those of the publisher. The publisher therefore disclaims responsibility for the views or opinions expressed within the work.

All quotes, unless otherwise noted, are from the New King James Version. Copyright 1979, 1980, 1982 by Thomas Nelson, Inc. Used by permission. All rights reserved.

Scriptures marked NIV are taken from the HOLY BIBLE, NEW INTERNATIONAL VERSION,. Copyright © 1973, 1978, 1984 by International Bible Society. Used by permission of Zondervan Publishing House. All rights reserved.

Scriptures marked KJV are taken from The Holy Bible, King James Version. Copyright © 1972 by Thomas Nelson Inc., Camden, New Jersey 08103.

ESV® Text Edition: 2011.

Paperback ISBN-13: 978-1-66288-277-7
Ebook ISBN-13: 978-1-66288-278-4

Table of Contents

Introduction vii

Christian Songs. 1
#1–I'm Ready to Meet My Savior in Heaven 1
#2–Now I Know the Truth. 2
#3–Hallelujah, Hallelujah, Hallelujah 4
#4 – I am Not Ashamed to Call You My God 6
#5 – I Owe You Thanks 8

Country Songs 15
#6–Country. 15
#7 – Born a Redneck 18
#8 – Common Sense 21
#9 – Our Wedding Day 23
#10 – Pool of Love 25
#11 – Forever Love. 28

Love Songs 33
#12 – Your Magic Touch 35
#13 – My Girl Is a Love Maker Teacher 36
#14 – Respect, Appreciate, Work Together. 38
#15 – Celebrate Every Day. .42

#16 – You Can Call Me 45
#17 – Meaning of Family 49
#18 – The Perfect Match 52
#19 – Father's Day 55

God Songs. 59
#20 – God's Army 59
#21 – Why Hasn't God Answered My Prayers? 62
#22 – I Am Blessed 64
#23 – God Please Give Me a Sign. 67
#24 – What Would I Do If…? .69
#25 – Your Name Is Beautiful .70
#26 – I Promised Myself. 72
#27–My Life Became a Diamond. 74
#28 – The Power of Prayers 76
#29 – Christmas. 78
#30 – You Can Fly Higher Than an Eagle 83
#31 – I'm Proud to be an American 86

Introduction

I wrote this book of songs to share my knowledge with everyone around the world, not to get rich or famous. This has been my dream. Writers like me write books to share our thoughts with everyone. When you read this book, you have a few good options. You can use our knowledge to make you a better person and develop your mind. George Speck was the one who invented the first potato chip. How many companies have used the same idea in different ways? I just want you to know the world is waiting for you to share your own ideas. Never give up trying. The harder you fall, the stronger can become if you get back up on your feet. Don't let anyone limit your goals, including yourself. Use both your mind and your heart together as they work together to lead you in the same direction so there is no confusion. Don't forget failure means you just need more knowledge, more ways, and more options. You are the only one who knows what your goals, dreams, talents, and knowledge mean to you. Share what you have learned and learn from others as well.

You shouldn't let anyone make you doubt yourself.

The message in these songs is for all people around the world. It doesn't matter who you are or where you come from.

I'm Haitian, but after twenty-two years in America with all the different races and nationalities, my knowledge of different cultures has grown and open my mind to the value each one brings.

We all have minds, but we use our minds differently. For example, when we read the Bible, we all understand it in a different way. We have a lot of things in common as well. We need to celebrate our differences, not speak or act badly to one another.

Sometimes, we think we know what is best for our kids, families, countries, races, and nations. However, we should never forget we are connected together as members of the human race.

Perhaps, the one you think is your worst enemy, may desire to learn from you and be your best friend. We need to learn from each other to make our knowledge grow. Our problem is we see others do things we don't understand so we criticize or even fear them.

Be aware of how television can corrupt your mind. What you feed your mind can distort what you know in your heart is true or false, right or wrong. If you really watch television with the right mindset, you will be able to learn and understand your world better.

You should continually seek to know why you are here on earth. Think about what you need to do to make yourself and the world better. If you can't help yourself achieve a better life, there is no way you will be able to help someone else. You must understand yourself in order to understand and help others.

The best way to learn and grow is to not judge others by the color of their skin or where they came from. I understand

Indians don't look like black people, and Chinese don't look like white people. However, we can all work together to improve our world. Our love should be unconditional and not based on color, race, or religion.

A country like Ukraine shouldn't be in the situation it's in right now. Our world should seek to achieve peace not allow one government or country to start a war. It is time for all the governments around the world to sit down and have a meeting to stop this nonsense. The only way for a country to be taken by another country is if the citizens and the government of the country ask for help like Puerto Rico and America. I can't understand why the world lets one man destroy world peace.

The most important thing you can learn from these examples is you should walk through life expecting to grow, improve, and help others do the same. You should never let life's events walk over or through you. Use common sense as you walk through each day. Common sense works the same way your body does. You will always know when you use a part of your body wrong. If something keeps you from moving forward, you are doing something wrong. It is very easy to figure it out and fix it.

Greed

Greed is a "disease" in our world tearing us apart instead of helping us to move forward to world peace. We need to find a way to resolve this problem.

Ask Yourself…

Are you reaching for more than you need?

Are you going to use the extra blessings you receive all for yourself or to help others?

Are you going to be happy with more or will you be constantly worrying someone will take it from you?

My grandma used to say, "You always need to put your hat where you can reach it."

This is one of the reasons I never eat more than my stomach can digest comfortably. I never bite off more than I can chew.

When you read the Bible, you should be able to explain and describe God to others based on what you have learned.

Ask Yourself…

Why is it we can describe Jesus and His Father, but we can't describe ourselves?

How can we call ourselves Christians if we do not act like Christ?

Do we believe as long as we go to church, we are Christians?

True Christians are the ones who choose to follow the rules of God. Be careful as you seek the truth. You need to be willing to apply God's truth to yourself even if it hurts.

It is a shame to see the way human beings are behaving toward each other. We only seek knowledge about things we want to understand. However, it is becoming obvious why our planet is now a living hell for many people.

Never let anyone tell you your value and make you think they are better than you.

It is time to understand having more money than others doesn't mean someone is better than others. We all have a copy of the blueprint of life in our hands. We can design it however we want if we know how to use our common sense. It makes sense a positive mindset brings positive energy.

Do you really want to always feel like you are missing something in your life or are you ready to be complete?

My prayer is these songs will start you on the road to a whole and prosperous life through following God's blueprint for your life.

Note: This book of songs is for people twenty-one and older. Even though I don't use bad words, you still shouldn't let them read it without you reading it first to see if a song is right for them.

Rules and Vital Information about my Book of Songs

It is important to read this note before reading this book. I wrote this book to share with everyone around the world who wants to try it. However, all these rules must be followed.

First, you can work with any song, but you will need to claim it on my website.[1] Then, I will let you work with the

---

[1] Include website information

song for three months. If you need more time, you need to let me know. If not, the song will be back on the market.

When you know for sure you want to use the song, you will sign the contract with a small percentage like a donation and then you can change the song however you want.

You can add or take away whatever phrases you want and even though some songs already tell which type of songs they are, you can use them for any type of song you prefer.

However, if you use my songs without my permission, I will claim every penny you make and you will be sued for not following the rules.

I hope everyone is happy with my songs and uses them as instructed. It is a book for everyone and includes Christian songs, country songs, love songs, hip-hop, rap, etc. Enjoy!

Christian Songs

#1–I'm Ready to Meet My Savior in Heaven

I'm ready, I'm ready, I'm ready
to meet my savior in heaven.

Repeat.

What makes you think that you are ready?
I'm ready because I know and follow
God's Ten Commandments.

What are the Ten Commandments?

First: Love God with all your heart.
Second: Worship only God.
Third: Always say God's name
with love and respect.
Fourth: Honor the Lord by resting
on the seventh day.
Fifth: Love and respect your parents.
Sixth: Never hurt anyone.
Seventh: Keep wedding promises.
Eighth: Don't steal.

Nineth: You need to always tell the truth.
Tenth: Be happy with what you have and
don't wish for other people's stuff.

Oh yes, you are definitely ready
to meet our Father God in heaven.

One more time.

#2–Now I Know the Truth

I didn't know what I was looking for.
But now, I have found the truth
and I will be the truth.

Repeat.

I used to walk with my head down
never looking up, but right now,
I will be the person I was born to be.
You are my Savior and
I will always honor You, my God.

Now I know what is good about the Lord.
I'm not going back. I'm not going back.

Repeat.

I remember the day I wanted someone
just to talk to and understand my situation.
I couldn't find one, I couldn't find one.

Since I met You, Lord,
You haven't left me for a second of my life.
A second of my life.
I honor my Lord; I honor my Father.

Now I know what I should do to follow the rules of God.
I'm not going back.
I'm not going back.

Now I know how powerful prayers are.
I'm not going back. I'm not going back.

I know the source of love from You my Father God and
I'm not going to stay a day
without soaking in your love,
soaking in the truth of life.

I'm not going to stay a day
without soaking in your love,
soaking in the truth of life.
Every single day, I look at myself
as the most blessed person alive.

Now I can see the value of Your presence, God.
I'm not going back. I'm not going back.

Now I know how to receive my blessings
from You God. I'm not going back.
I'm not going back.

#3–Hallelujah, Hallelujah, Hallelujah

Hallelujah, Hallelujah, Hallelujah
I received my blessing from the Lord
by following the rules of God.
If you don't know, I can tell you how.

Hallelujah, Hallelujah, Hallelujah
I received the blessing of God
by following the Ten Commandments.
If you don't know, I can show you how.

Your life becomes how you treat it.
If you treat it as a joke, it could be a joke.
But if you treat it as the most important
thing you need to focus on,
it can become an amazing journey.
Our God doesn't choose who
He thinks should have a good life.
We are all born with a different direction of life. But it
doesn't mean the Lord chooses
who is to be rich or poor.
We just need to follow God's direction
for our life and His rules, the right way.
Then it doesn't matter what happens.
You know you always have someone
with you even though you can't see Him.
He is the only one who
says yes and means it.

Hallelujah, Hallelujah, Hallelujah

I received my blessing from the Lord
by following the rules of God.
If you don't know, I can tell you how.

Hallelujah, Hallelujah, Hallelujah
I received the blessing of God
by following the Ten Commandments.
If you don't know, I can show you how.

Human beings want things done overnight.
Our God is true, faithful, and real.
The Lord's prayer is very powerful.
You need to know how it works.
You need to pray and believe
what God has promised us.
He said, "The ones who believe in God
are the ones who believe in themselves.
The ones who continually receive My blessings
are those who are true to themselves and others. You are
true and strong in My presence
and your blessings are from things
you do and how you do them.
Keep up the good work and be patient,
and your blessing will come.

Hallelujah, Hallelujah, Hallelujah
I received my blessing from the Lord
by following the rules of God.
If you don't know, I can tell you how.

Hallelujah, Hallelujah, Hallelujah

I received the blessing of God
by following the Ten Commandments.
If you don't know, I can show you how.

#4 – I am Not Ashamed to Call You my God

I can see my life getting better day by day.
I can see my mindset is in the right direction.
I can see and understand what life is about. Today, want
to thank You for all the things
You have done for me, God.

You are my savior.
You are my strength.
You are my Lord.
Anywhere I go, I will not be ashamed
to call You, my God.

I remember who I was and where I came from. Though
You said to leave the past in the past, when I think about
where I was,
I see I became stronger being with You.
I believe all You have said in Your Word. "When you hurt
others, you hurt yourself more.
The one who believes in Me is
the one who follows My rules.
Don't try to fool yourself
and think you fool Me.
I'm your creator,
I know everything you do, good and bad.

I can see my life getting better day by day.
I can see my mindset is in the right direction.
I can see and understand what life is about. Today, want
to thank You for all the things
You have done for me, God.

You are my savior.
You are my strength.
You are my Lord.
Anywhere I go, I will not be ashamed
to call You my God.

Lord, I have a few questions for You.
Are we all the same as we are human beings?
Don't You love all of us the same way?
Do You have two ways of going to heaven?
What can we do to end the war between us?

I can see my life getting better day by day.
I can see my mindset is in the right direction.
I can see and understand what life is about. Today, want
to thank You for all the things
You have done for me, God.

You are my savior.
You are my strength.
You are my Lord.
Anywhere I go, I will not be ashamed
to call You my God.

Thank You, Father, for the life I have.

I have questions for my brothers and sisters.
Are we going to make our world
a heavenly place to live?
Do we really love our kids and wish
to leave them a better world than ours?
Are we going to work together to
make our world a heavenly place to live
and receive the blessing of God?
What is the most important thing in life?
Are you ready to meet me part way?

I can see my life getting better day by day.
I can see my mindset is in the right direction.
I can see and understand what life is about. Today, want
to thank You for all the things
You have done for me, God.

You are my savior.
You are my strength.
You are my Lord.
Anywhere I go, I will not be ashamed
to call You my God.

#5 – I Owe You Thanks

If today I am alive,
I owe You thanks.
If today I'm beautiful,
I owe You thanks.
You don't like us to be greedy,
But I can't get enough of You,

my God.

If I'm on my feet,
I owe You thanks.
If I have a great life,
I owe You thanks
You don't like us to be greedy,
But I can't get enough of You,
my God.

You gave me life
You brought me
happiness and peace.
What can I do to show You
I appreciate You are my God?

You brought me strength
to win over my enemies.
You brought me enough love for me and to share
with others.
What can I do to show You
I appreciate You are my God?

If today I am alive,
I owe You thanks.
If today I'm beautiful,
I owe You thanks.
You don't like us to be greedy,
But I can't get enough of You,
my God.

If I'm on my feet,
I owe You thanks.
If I have a great life,
I owe You thanks
You don't like us to be greedy,
But I can't get enough of You,
my God.

You said, "Give but don't expect anything in return."
You said, "Love should be the best gift to share with
each other."
You said, "Every life matters."

Why don't we listen to You?
Why don't we do things right?

You said we should be united.
You said we should be true
to each other.
You said we should have each other's backs.

Why don't we listen to You?
Why don't we do things right?

If today I am alive,
I owe You thanks.
If today I'm beautiful,
I owe You thanks.
You don't like us to be greedy,
But I can't get enough of You,
my God.

> If I'm on my feet,
> I owe You thanks.
> If I have a great life,
> I owe You thanks
> You don't like us to be greedy,
> But I can't get enough of You,
> my God.

Pause and Reflect…

I can see Christians are going into a different type of world today, where we will never reach our destination. I wish I understood the direction we are head. Is it our destiny or tradition?

Every way has a start and an end. I wish I could know where and when our direction will end.

Here are some important questions we all need to answer:

What is the meaning of being a Christians?

If the worker represents the company, who do we represent?

Do we need to wait until we get to heaven to enjoy life, or we should start it from here?

What is the purpose of going to church if we are not following God's rules?

Who is God and what should we do to receive His blessings?

Please, if you know the answers to my questions, please help me out and send me your answers.

Christians should be an example to the world of who God is and how to receive His blessings. However, it seems we are the ones who destroy and divide the world the most.

We should be the happiest set of people in this world, yet we are the most unhappy.

Blessings should fall in our lives first, but we are the last ones who ever see and acknowledge our blessings.

We want to share with others about the Lord, yet we never really invite Him into our lives.

We live unhappy and unhealthy lifestyles, full of lies and greed. We don't understand why we are the last ones on the Lord's list for blessings.

We know the truth and we know what is false. We know what is right and we know what is wrong. So, why do we keep making false steps and doing what we know is wrong? We should understand when we make mistakes and do foolish things, the Lord already sees it. Our Father God wants us to earnestly seek forgiveness and be willing to learn from our mistake but also make changes. We should not be going back to God repeatedly asking for forgiveness for the same things.

Why do we human beings always want it the hard way?

Important Message

I'm not trying to tell anyone how to live their lives. However, we all know what we really need to do is to make our world a better place to live. I'm ready to do my best to get my part done right and I hope you are, too. This world is our home. The main reason it is going downhill so destructively is because of wrong information. We have been blaming various people and governments, but the truth is, it is time for us to blame ourselves for the things we have done or not done. It is time for us to give the credit to the one who deserves it.

I know that I was born perfect just like everyone else. I know each of us has our own destination of life. I don't expect anyone to do the things I do, and no one should expect me to do things they do. It shouldn't keep us from learning from each other. We need to understand it is not about blaming God or even Satan. It is about us and our families following the rules of life. We should start right now and see how much we can do for our kids and our next generation.

I know I was born with a purpose, and I have my free will which makes me able to do whatever things I want. If I choose to do things the wrong way, I should take responsibility and pay the consequences of my actions. I will not have anyone else to blame but myself.

Listen, life is so good and beautiful. Let's choose to do things right and enjoy every second of it before we end our life on this earth. I love to read the Bible. I can see the truth choose to apply what's relevant to me and my life.

Christians, we were born to be partners with each other. Often, we want to lead and have others follow us, but we don't want to follow anyone else. If we think we know everything, we just fool ourselves. This is how simple life is. The Lord worked very hard to build us a wonderful world and we destroyed it. Now, we are waiting for Him to fix it.

We need to understand Who we represent. What we should do is to make others know we are Christians without them asking us questions. The word Christian is not a label for people who go to Baptist church or any other denominational or non-denominational church. It is for everyone who believes in God and choose to follow the rules of God.

I love you all and I don't expect you to be perfect. However, we can do it better if we choose to. Enjoy reading this book of songs.

Country Songs

Introduction

I wrote these country songs to share my knowledge with you. We all know the truth. We should accept it and it shouldn't matter who or where it comes from. Our world needs us, and we should work together to make it the best place to live.

#6–Country

The way I love my life is on a Friday night
there is nothing better than sitting down in a bar
and watching your favorite games on TV
with a cold beer in your hands; with a cold beer in
your hands.
One day, I asked my mom, what is good about rednecks?
She told me, "There are two different types of rednecks,
a good one and a bad one.
A real redneck never takes advantage of others,
is ready to work as one nation,
and support each other no matter how bad the weather is.
We never let anyone take away what belongs to us.

We are always on the go, always try to finish whatever we start,
by making anything with everything we have.
We are ones who always puts their families first.
in everything including life."
Then she said, "If you don't know who is a real redneck,
you are looking at one; you are looking at one.
I'm a redneck woman who will always be a redneck."

If I knew all these good things about rednecks before,
I could have appreciated being a redneck.
better than I do right now; better than I do right now.

I remember when I was seventeen, I had my first beer.
My dad didn't tell me how the taste would be,
but the circumstances and what could happen if I
used it wrong.
One Friday night before my dad went to the bar,
I asked him what was good about hanging out with red-
neck friends,
He said son, "There is no one who you can trust better
than a redneck,
We always have each other's back and it doesn't matter
what happens.
It is not easy to get to know a redneck.
But when you do, you will never want to let us go.
We always think positively with positive hopes,
even though we don't know when it will happen.
We are always proud of ourselves.
We believe in forgiveness and starting over brand new.
and dropping everything that happened in the past.

If you really want love and respect,
the best place to find them is in a redneck's heart.
A real redneck doesn't usually tell anyone he loves them,
he shows them the best love they have for them.

If you want to know who a redneck is.
You are looking at one; you are looking at one.
A redneck who is proud to be a redneck
from the day he was born; from the day he was born.

If I knew all these good things about rednecks before,
I could have appreciated being a redneck.
better than I do right now; better than I do right now.

One Sunday evening, I saw my grandpa dressed in his
cowboy dress.
I asked him what was fun about enjoying life as a cowboy.
He told me, "I believe no one can enjoy themselves better
than rednecks.
We believe life is made to enjoy.
We bring our family to different places of joy,
We like being a cowboy,
and seal our families together with the glue of love.
We always believe families come first.
There are many who don't know what rednecks are about.
But we know exactly what we're about.
It is so easy to know a real redneck the first time you meet.
When we say yes, we mean it and we never try to break
our promises,
especially when it comes to our families.
When I see a real redneck, I realize it before he even talks.

If you have never seen a redneck before,
right now, you are looking at one; you are looking at one.
A redneck who knows the true meaning of redneck.
A redneck who knows the true meaning of redneck.
I'm a redneck who is proud to be a redneck.

If I knew all these good things about rednecks before,
I could have appreciated being a redneck.
better than I do right now; better than I do right now.

#7 – Born a Redneck

You love to be who you are.
I love to be a redneck.
We all are from different nations and races.
Each of us has our own culture.
It doesn't matter where we are from.
We all have good and bad things about us.
We can't judge who to point our fingers at.
We all have something special about us.
We all are racist in different ways.
We need to try to understand why we are racist.
We prefer to hide being racist like it was a crime.

My dad used to tell me, "When someone
wants to stop you from doing something good,
use it as a positive energy to stick to your plan.
You may not know where you will be.
But you always need to know exactly who you are."

I was born a redneck. I grew up a redneck.

It doesn't matter what anyone says,
I love to be a redneck.
It makes me feel special every single day of my life.

If redneck mean racist,
Texas would be the most racist state in America.
We don't just listen to everything someone says.
We use common sense before we believe what is
false for true.

I remember when I was a young boy, my father used
to tell me.
"Son, a man is the one who can build a good life for
their family.
A real redneck is always wearing non-slip shoes.
to make sure he doesn't say oops.
You should always love yourself before anyone else.
That will show you how to love others in the right way.
Don't forget, we don't find love, love finds us.
When it wants to go, it will disappear like it was
never there.
I can't teach you something you don't want to know.
If you really want to be a redneck, you just need to be
real about it.
This is our tradition, and we want to keep it real.
Then pass it on the same way our parents passed it on to us.

If rednecks mean racist, Texas would be the most racist
state in America.
This is why you don't just listen to everything someone says.

Use your common sense before you believe what is false for true.

"Son, you never feel the taste of winning until you lose. When you fail," Mom said, "you learn to be a strong winner.
When you fail, you learn to be stronger, not to be a quitter.
Never think something is too easy until you have it done."

Cowboys always learn things the hard way.
By the time they realize it,
We already know a thousand ways to do it.
We think a thousand times and try to do it once.
If we don't, there is no way we will do it a third time.
This is one of the reasons we enjoy everything we do.
We try to put passion in the way we do things.
We sometimes do things others think are stupid.
We never think of the stupid things they have done.
Cowboys learn how to hold tight before swinging.
You can't explain yourself to someone who doesn't know who he is.
Don't wait for the right time,
You just need to let time catch up on your way of life.
By the time you realize it. You are already ahead of time.
This is one of the reasons rednecks will always be rednecks.
and cowboys will always be cowboys.

If redneck mean racist,
Texas would be the most racist state in America.
We don't just listen to everything someone says.

We use common sense before we believe what is
false for true.

Everyone who is proud to be a redneck, come out here.
Women to the right and men to the left.
Two steps forward and two steps backwards
Turn around with two quick moves,
Put a big smile on your face and show you're proud to be
a redneck.

#8 – Common Sense

Today, I want to share this message with you.
All I really want is for you to understand my point of view.
We all have a brain that comes with common sense.
We should do our best to make them work right.
We know all the things that are good to do
and things that are bad, too.
We should try to connect our minds to increase our
knowledge,
Feel each other's pain, and then find ways to cure them,
With no attention to race, religion, and culture.

What are we doing to find the solution?
When do our lives become something of worth?
This is not about black and white or yellow and green.
We know what to do to get to the bottom of our problems.
We should not wait; we should not wait,
we should not wait to see another generation inherit
this mess.
We should try our best to clean it up as soon as possible.

The Reality of Life

If we really want to do it, we can, yes we can.
If we really want to do it, we can, yes we can.

The ones who serve us faithfully are the ones we treat badly.
Our soldiers should have a special spot in our hearts.
After all the things they go through to keep us safe
We don't even give them a little appreciation.
They gave away their freedom,
So, we can have ours with a peace of mind.
They gave up their lives and time with their families.
After all the things they went through, when they come back,
They should be able to enjoy every second of their life,
But instead, no one seems to care about them.
Some end up in the streets begging and homeless.

What are we doing to find the solution
where our soldiers' lives can be worth our care?
This is not about black and white or yellow and green.
We know what to do to get to the bottom of our problems.
We should not, no we should not wait, no we should not wait,
We should not wait to see another soldier homeless on the street.
We should try to do something about it as soon as possible.
If we really want to do it, we can, yes, we can.
If we really want to do it, we can, yes, we can.

I wish we would each look at ourselves in the mirror.
So we can see how we look right now.
We scare our own souls.

I wish we would all wake up.
And see it is time to change our lives.
If we don't, we have no one to blame but ourselves.

What are we doing to find the solution
where our lives can be worth the same?
This is not about black and white or yellow and green.
We know what to do to get to the bottom of our problems.
We should not, we should not wait, no, we should not wait,
we should not wait to see another generation inherit
this mess.
We should try our best to clean it up as soon as possible.
If we really want to do it, we can, yes, we can.
If we really want to do it, we can, yes, we can.

#9 – Our Wedding Day

Today is my last day to live the wild life.
I have made a commitment to my girl.
Baby, I know the good life you deserve.
I'm ready to make your dream come true.
To make you the happiest girl in town.
I know we have been in this relationship for a while.
We have learned how to grow a healthy love between us.
It was good to learn the good and the bad things about us.
Right now, we know each other exactly the way we should.
I know this step is the best step I've ever taken.
I know we will never regret it.

This is the day for us to get married and leave all the fornication behind.

I can't wait to see us walk up the aisle and begin to call
you, my wife.
Baby, baby, baby, you know how much I really love you.
I'm ready to spend the rest of my life with you.
So, girl, our fornication ends tonight; girl, our fornication
ends tonight.

I truly believe no one can love me the way you do, baby.
We talk to each other like it was any fun activity in
our lives.
We don't let anything come between us.
We have our lives just the way we want.
I don't know if you are ready,
But I can't wait to discover the mystery of our lives.
I can't wait to see us walk down the aisle.
I will put the ring on your finger,
with a big smile and the words, I do.
We are going to be husband and wife.
We should never let anything go through our minds
To prevent our tree of love from growing.
We know there are two ways we can willingly enjoy it,
before we have kids and after our kids get older
and fly away.

This is the day for us to get married and leave all the fornication behind.
I can't wait to see us walk up the aisle and begin to call
you, my wife.
Baby, baby, baby, you know how much I really love you.
I'm ready to spend the rest of my life with you.

So, girl, our fornication ends tonight; girl, our fornication ends tonight.

I have a lot of things I learned from you I will never forget.
I remember when you talked about the one who is in poverty.
You said being rich doesn't have anything to do with money.
The one who is truly rich is the one who is happy.
I used to pass by where you live just to see your pretty face.
If I did not see your face, there were no good dreams.
Sometimes, when I remember how much I love you.
My emotions become super sensitive,
All I can do is call you just to hear your voice.
This is the day for us to get married and leave all the fornication behind.
I can't wait to see us walk up the aisle and begin to call you, my wife.
Baby, baby, baby, you know how much I really love you.
I'm ready to spend the rest of my life with you.
So, girl, our fornication ends tonight; girl, our fornication ends tonight.

#10 – Pool of Love

Welcome to the redneck bar.
Tonight, we have everything on special.
You buy one drink and get one for free.
Redneck members have a free margarita.
with a slice of pineapple on the side.
Gils and guys get ready.

You know what cowboys are all about.
You look innocent and I look like a cowboy.
Baby, please sit right here and let me have a minute of your time.

I can make you dream of swimming in the pool of love.
Beautiful flowerpots are all over the place.
Filled with amazing boutiques of flowers.
You hear continuous melodious songs.
Filled with only phrases of love.
Wine is on the table beside you.
And snacks of your choice.
It was a dream come true.
This is what I am about.
This is what I'm about.

Honey, you are so beautiful, let me hold your hand.
You might know the direction of life,
But I don't think you know the direction of love.
I'm not here to fool you or take anything from you.
I want to show you what I'm about,
by showing the world of love not the life you had before.
I know you have probably been there and done them all.
But I know a place you have never been before.
The heavenly goodness of immeasurable and unlimited love.
Baby, let me do the honor to be the first one who shows you there.
I am the man who will make you reach there safe and sound.
I am the man for it; I am the man for it.

I can make you dream of swimming in the pool of love.
Beautiful flowerpots are all over the place.
Filled with amazing boutiques of flowers.
You hear continuous melodious songs.
Filled with only phrases of love.
Wine is on the table beside you.
And snacks of your choice.
It was a dream come true.
This is what I am about.
This is what I'm about.

Sweetheart, you already know how us rednecks do.
You don't need to be ashamed.
Let me hold your hand and take you there.
I know where love is and I know what you are
going to gain.
All you need is to trust and believe me knowing I could
never hurt you.
That would be the last thing I would ever want to do.
I don't know or do everything a cowboy does.
But I can show you the direction our love can take.
Just like a piece of cake with a bottle of wine
without glasses
Ready to lay back and float. This is what I am about.

I can make you dream of swimming in the pool of love.
Beautiful flowerpots are all over the place.
Filled with amazing boutiques of flowers.
You hear continuous melodious songs.
Filled with only phrases of love.
Wine is on the table beside you.

And snacks of your choice.
It was a dream come true.
This is what I am about.
This is what I'm about.

#11 – Forever Love

My guitar has one string, and my song only has one word,
But I have enough to make you feel special,
Every single day of your life.
I try to pull you up with me,
But you are always trying to run away from me.
I don't understand why you can't see,
I'm the man who will walk you to the hill top?
Baby, if it is a mistake to love you,
I'm ready to make this mistake for the rest of my life.
Without you, the sun doesn't rise.
The rain doesn't fall in the garden of my life.
Baby, my mind thinks about you like a space shuttle going into space.
I can't understand why you can't see I'm the man who is right for you.

My baby girl, mi amor, ma Cherie, I just want you to know,
If there is one girl in this world I love, it's you, only you.
You are the only one who makes me dream of forever love.

Every time I think about eternal love,
You are the first and last one I see in the picture.
Every time I think about love. I feel drowsy and sick.

Even though I don't really know your name.
Is it Mary, Maria, or Marie?
Every time I call one of them, my prayers are answered.
I know the level I can reach from love.
I'm not afraid to use it for you.
I'm ready to climb up any mountain.
Even with bare hands to find you.
I will never stop until the last breath of my life.
You always bring me good feelings,
And give me good energy,
Which makes my day end up beautiful.

My baby girl, mi amor, ma Cherie, I just want
you to know,
If there is one girl in this world I love, it's you: only you.
You are the only one who makes me dream of forever love.

Baby, I see my whole life dreaming about you
being my wife.
Cooking and cleaning for you and all you ever need.
I want to make you feel like my royal queen and see
you happy.
This is what you call love!
I have so many good thoughts.
I am thinking about our love relationship.
These are the things for us to talk about.
We need to share our thoughts and ideas.
Please, don't let me be the one to get it done, alone.
Last night, I dreamed we were together,
We were enjoying our beautiful love,
But you were not yet my wife.

Please baby, let this last part of my dream come true.
All I really need is for you to make my dream become reality.
Just make my dream of love together become reality.
This treasure of my love is waiting just for you and nobody else.

My baby girl, mi amor, ma Cherie, I just want you to know,
If there is one girl in this world I love, it's you, only you.
You are the only one who makes me dream of forever love.

Important Message

This message is for all people who live around the world. My name is Hubert Severe and I'm Haitian. I'm very proud to be who I am. I just want to share my knowledge with you. This world is our world, but it is divided, and no one wants to put it together because of selfishness.

No one wants anyone to come to their countries and do whatever they want. Anyone who enters another country should follow the rules of the country. Immigrants want to go to other countries, but they want to do things their way. If immigrants come into your country, they should be treated like all your fellow citizens, whether they are black, white, or yellow.

We all should choose to be faithful to work together to move our country in the right direction of life without thinking of what other people say. Our world is in danger because of negligence, greed, and taking advantage of others who are kind.

For example: My Haitian brothers and sisters are connecting and should help each other, but we should never think of taking advantage of each other. We have millions of Haitian people who live in other countries all over the world. They have left Haiti and no longer care about their former country. Please, my brothers and sisters, you are smart so don't let greed and selfishness keep you from doing good. Please be smart and be kind, and the Lord will be with you. When you pretend to be good, the Lord will laugh at you and consider you foolish.

Welcome to America. The greatest country in the world, but it has the most people living on the streets who don't have anything, why? It is because of selfishness and greed. It is time we work together to help solve this problem.

Pause and Reflect…

Are there people living on the street in your city or town?

What do you think can be done about it?

Think of ways you might be able to work with others to help this situation in some way.

Important Message

America is one of the most loving countries around the world. I love this country. The United States of America is an amazing country as are their citizens.

Immigrants have more respect in the USA than some of the citizens of their own country, *true or false*. You can see and hear the way the world talks about America including people who use the goodness of America. I just want you to know you have a great country with great people.

However, life has its rules. I understand the word freedom, but some of the ways you are doing things to make others happy allows some people destroy your reputation. I know there are men, women, gays, and lesbians living in this country. Unless they are breaking the law, the government should not be involved in their personal lives. Please America, you are the head of the world, and the world needs you to disregard every non-essential thing and concentrate on what is best for your citizens. It starts with you. Thank you.

Love Songs

Important Message

    We all know there are two types of people. There are men and women. Even though we divide by different races, religions, color, and sex, we all are human beings. We should love ourselves, but not or more than we love others. You can never be happy and feel love the way you should be living lonely. Am I right? We all need people around us even though we dislike them, or they are our worst enemies. Life doesn't mean living alone and isolated. It means you commit to challenge yourself and all the others who live around you. When you pass the test is when you do your best to move on to the next level of the game until the last ones and you know some of them will fail. You should not be the reason and you should not be worried about it either because you know we all have our own destination in life. When you take a good look at life, you will see life says one plus one equals two, one minus one equals one, and one divided by one equals one. You should use your common sense and know the right answer before you see yourself in the opposite of the ways.

    Sometimes, we need to jump, sometimes we need to run, and sometimes we need to jump and run at the same time. Do you feel me? From the time we are born to our last day on earth is challenging. You have two ways of challenging yourself. Is to be the winner or be the loser? When you are the winner in life is when you follow the rules of life and it doesn't matter if you make it or not. You are the loser in life when you do bad things and you don't come forward and clear yourself about the things you did wrong. You continue your life with it like it is a good recipe and make others do it without warning them.

Why do people say the higher you fall from the harder you hit the floor. Instead, you should say the highest you can go will be with your Heavenly Father. Every single phrase has a definition. It can be good, and it can be bad in the same way. You are the one who should flip it all the different ways to find the right definition for it, nobody else's. Our lives could be sweet and sour or salty and bitter. We still can bring good life and happiness to our lives if we aren't selfish. True or false?

You should train a child to receive love, give love, and learn the meaning of love even though he or she probably does not haves the knowledge to understand like we do. This is one of the reasons our love fades away little by little. We don't understand we learn to share about not avoid troublesome things happening in our lives. The same holds true when we fail at something, especially when it comes to family. Our selfishness can get in the way, though. We know we can make our families always have a better quality of love, peace, and happiness, so, what are we waiting for. Everyday life is a gift, take it and make the best of it. Please don't forget, this is not a Bible. This is a book of songs for everyone to read.

I can see myself reaching another level as I write and sing these songs about love. I'm very happy I didn't let hard work make me quit. Now I'm celebrating my victory in life. Right now, I just want to share my experiences with the whole world. You shouldn't let anything get in your way when you want to reach your goals or your dreams of true love.

#12 – Your Magic Touch

Sweetheart, you know where we came from and I know it, too.
This isn't only our destiny, but our dream.
We knew we would be together,
But we just couldn't believe it could happen so fast.
The only thing we can think of is
Love each other and see each other happy.
Is no way we will do anything to break our promises.
We are already doing them all, good and bad.
We just need to keep doing things right.
Continue to wish never to be off track.
You love me and I love you.
I talked and you listened.
You make the rules and I follow them.
We have each other's rights on the target.
You taught me a lot of things I will never forget.
For example: Your magic touch.
When I saw you, I knew you were special.
Why do you shut me out with everything you do?

I saw you could be a teacher.
But I didn't think you'd be my love teacher.
Baby, I reward you with the best love I have.
The trophy will be my heart.

#13 – My Girl Is a Love Maker Teacher

My girl is a love maker teacher.
She taught me things I never thought existed.
She is a natural girl who comes with the whole package.
I will never leave her for anything.

Come on baby, hand-to-hand, face-to-face, and double lips on actions.
You know, I'm not lying and even the answer from your heart is yes.
I already forget where I came from due to this beautiful relationship we have.
I can't ever forget where we are and where we are going.
I didn't understand you until I started putting things into our relationship.
You are a girl who comes with a lot of love experiences, and for that, you have the best love my heartbeat can ever make.
I knew there was someone out there I could trust.
But I never thought she would be you.
Now I can understand why this smile stays on my face.
You make my heart pump faster
Now you make me the happiest man of all.
Look for the love you search for until you find it,
Then keep it and never let it go.
Please baby, finding good love and owning it is not an easy thing to do. Sweetheart, I cannot explain the way you make love explainable to me
Now I can understand when you said, make sure I find where I want to be.

Baby, you are the best stop I have ever made.
I will never walk away from this site, and you can trust me on this.

My girl is a love maker teacher.
She taught me things I never thought existed.
She is a natural girl who comes with the whole package.
I will never leave her for anything.

My angel from the sky, the Lord blessed me with you.
He dropped you in the palm of my hand,
I will take great care of my love and the way you do things,
Sometimes I think I am sleeping.
I thought, no one can dream of the enjoyment I have with you.
The Lord is my shepherd to help me keep our relationship perfect.
I've heard people talk about luck and blessings,
My belief starts with you and you know what I mean.
I know we live to forgive and forget.
I forgive you, but how can I forget your juicy kisses?
Your sweet eyes can twist my mind,
Your body language can make me never know where I am.
I would die before I'd leave you, baby.
What man can live without the clean oxygen of true love?
You have the best oxygen I have ever breathed in your love.
Baby, I understand many don't know the quality of good things.
But not me. When I see it. I know it. When I find it,
I keep it.
When I own it, I take great care of it.

I want to make it want to stay and never leave me.
I hope that's the way you feel.

My girl is a love maker teacher.
She taught me things I never thought existed.
She is a natural girl who comes with the whole package.
I will never leave her for anything.

#14 – Respect, Appreciate, Work Together

Honey, I know if one of us goes, we are going to leave each other behind.
Right now, we have the opportunity to be one in everything we do.
Let us take advantage of it to be the best couple ever.
You know we can do it if we really want to.
Make an effort and we can live like a happy couple.
Baby, let us leave all the bad moments in the past.
Let's bring the love life we always wish for into the present.
Mi amor, I love you so much, I will give up my life to save yours.
You are my princess. I will be your prince as long I live.
If you give me a chance, Sweetheart,
I will take my time and rebuild your love the way it should be.
Every drop of your love will be used for something good.
Our love relationship will be wonderful.
Nothing will come between us.
Your love was easy to fix. I can see you as the happiest woman alive.
If you can trust me and believe in me,

I truly believe I can do more for you with my love.
I can transform you to a different level.
I can show how a real man loves.
You and I will be lovey-dovey all the time.
No one can make you happy unless you choose to be.
I know I can do it and I already see how.
The only thing you need to do is to do your part.
Leave the rest for me to take care of.
Love involves respecting, appreciating, and
working together.
Without those ingredients, we will not be able to
grow our love.
This relationship is very special for both of us, my love.
You follow my lead, I'll follow your lead.
Many people thought we wouldn't last too long.
I believe we will be forever in love.
Don't worry baby, I've got your back.
It doesn't matter what happens in the future,
I will always take great care of you. That is my goal.

I remember when we just first met.
We didn't know what to say to each other.
We couldn't express our love to each other.
We just kept laughing at each other all the time.
We didn't realize we were in love.
We did things like kids will do.
We created ways to communicate.
People wouldn't know what we were about.
We continued with slow motion love.
Everyone says love is blind and we were for a time.
Even though we were blind, you talked and I laughed,

The Reality of Life

You said, why, and I said, I didn't know, then you'd laugh.
Who would think we could build a perfect relationship
From doing things other people think are stupid.
Baby, we built our love from things we love to do.
We believed in the way we were without copying other people's styles.
The thing we should do now is leave our relationship in God's hands.
Put Him in control by following His rules of love.
We can make it from where we are.
It will be easier to continue if we just choose to stay on track.
Baby, dreams can become reality.
But reality can never become a dream.
Let us keep things interesting and simple.
Separate things into two baskets.
Good goes to one and bad goes to the other.
We keep all the good ones and throw out all the bad ones.
Now, we can see how blessed relationships are built.

Love involves respecting, appreciating, and working together.
Without them, we will not be able to grow our love.
This relationship is very special for both of us, my love.
You follow my lead, I'll follow your lead.
Many people thought we wouldn't last too long.
I believe we will be forever in love.
Don't worry baby, I've got your back.
It doesn't matter what happens in the future,
I will always take great care of you. That is my goal.

Baby, you know how far we have come with this life.
Hot and cold weather and severe storms didn't stop us.
I'm not going to say we had the best relationship,
But our relationship is one in a million.
When I said I could make love manifest in your life,
You thought it was a joke.
Then, you saw I meant it by serving you candle-light dinners.
A bed full of flowers and special love making with juicy kisses.
You knew I didn't play when it comes to loving you.
Treating you the way I did when we just met.
Baby, I know you and I never need to worry
Something could happen to our relationship.
You are the most important thing in my life, and you always will be.
Love can walk in and walk out, but our love is our destiny.
I love you with a permanent love. It cannot be deleted or erased.
I love you girl!

Love involves respecting, appreciating, and working together.
Without them, we will not be able to grow our love.
This relationship is very special for both of us, my love.
You follow my lead, I'll follow your lead.
Many people thought we wouldn't last too long.
I believe we will be forever in love.
Don't worry baby, I've got your back.
It doesn't matter what happens in the future,
I will always take great care of you. That is my goal.

#15 – Celebrate Every Day

Are you coming, love?
If you don't want to come, it's all right.
No one should force you to take what you don't want.
However, your opportunity comes once in a lifetime.
If I were you, I wouldn't want to miss it for anyone.

You said you were over him.
But all you do shows me you still want to be with him.
You keep saying all the things he has done in your life.
You never see all the good things I have done for you.
All you can see are the women with good relationships.
I don't want you to keep lying to yourself.
If you don't really want to ride with me, just let me know.
Life is too short to worry about others who don't even know I exist.
Love can be found anywhere you wish or believe.
I feel so bad for telling you all these things. But guess what?
This is how it is, take it or leave it if it is too hot for you.
There is one thing you need to always know about life.
You need to fix your bed before you get sleepy.
Birds never fly unless they are ready.
Sometimes, they still need someone to teach them how.
Some of them aren't lucky enough to have someone to teach them.
They seek other's input to do it.
I will never hurt you or see you cry.
One last thing, l love you.
You should trust this love because it is real.

Girl, I can take you where happiness, love, respect, appreciation are.
I can take you where true love is if you give me a chance.
I will treat you as my royal queen.
Baby, you are my love.
I will not do anything to hurt you.
Our love will be forever love.

You keep saying you are unlucky, and God hates you,
You don't know what you have done.
You stress all the time, and you wish you were dead.
You should appreciate the wonderful life you have.
You should realize things happen for a reason.
This is the way life works.
You should appreciate how the Lord has blessed you.
The one you are already blessed with is with you.
He can turn out to be the one you wished for.
You should be happy and enjoy every second of your life.
You only have one life.
You shouldn't waste your time on people who
don't want you.

You are so cute and sweet in your own way.
You are special in a good way.
If you knew how, you would know your value.
I just want you to see where you are
You can turn to where you should be headed.
I know there is nothing impossible.
You and I can make this world into a better place.
Let us share what has made our lives a mystery to others.
No one ever did it the way we do.

Girl, I can take you where happiness, love, respect, appreciation are.
I can take you where true love is if you give me a chance.
I will treat you as my royal queen.
Baby, you are my love.
I will not do anything to hurt you.
Our love will be forever love.

Baby we always hear nothing lasts forever, but it is not true!
We can't tell when the world was made, or when it will be gone.
Right now, we each have the opportunity to beat the love system.
We daily show each other the real meaning of true love.
Our lives should be designed by the permanent marker of love.
We shouldn't try to delete or erase any of it.
We know today, but we don't know tomorrow.
Today is a gift from the Lord.
We should celebrate it like it is our last day on earth.

Girl, I can take you where happiness, love, respect, appreciation are.
I can take you where true love is if you give me a chance.
I will treat you as my royal queen.
Baby, you are my love.
I will not do anything to hurt you.
Our love will be forever love.

#16 – You Can Call Me

When you feel you need someone to talk to or
You need someone to keep you company,
You can call me, sweetheart.
When you feel you need someone to talk or
You need someone to keep you company,
You can call me, sweetheart.

Remember when we just met?
You needed someone to treat you right.
I looked like I could be right for the job.
We were friends for a while before we got in this relationship,
You trusted me with all your little secrets.
I did my best to keep them just the way you liked.
Baby I treated you just like we were husband and wife.
We didn't stay for a day without talking with each other.
I didn't think we could be more than just friends.
We have fun just like we were brother and sister.
We used to go out together, and watch TV together.
We did a lot of activities together like we were husband and wife.
We couldn't wait for our next day to start.
We used to dance, sing, and play all different types of games.
We didn't think those activities could grow our love inside of us.
I called you Sunflower and you called me Sunflower Seed.
It didn't matter where I was, just thinking of you kept me happy.

You and I used to be all for one and one for all.
There are a few things I can't ever get rid of in my life.
Your pretty face with the big smile,
Your sweet voice with the kindness of love and your body language.
Baby, I know there are some things we can't get control of.
But we can get control of ourselves.
Take a good look at yourself in the mirror.
There is no way you should want to look like someone else.
Love is a gift. Love works by giving it to the one who deserves it.
Erase and delete can mean the same thing.
But delete doesn't leave any stain behind, erase does.
This is why you should measure your love portion first
Before you mix it in everything you do.

When you feel you need someone to talk to or
You need someone to keep you company,
You can call me, sweetheart.
When you feel you need someone to talk or
You need someone to keep you company,
You can call me, sweetheart.

We started taking things seriously, you became completely different.
You want to control my life and treat me like I was your son.
You want to take all my freedom from me.
I love you with everything I've got, but I hate the emotions I feel.
We are all different and feel special just the way we are.

Love Songs

Our love can be upgraded, but not changed.
We should be happy to be just the way we are.
I love to help people, watch cartoons, and all other activities.
You want to take them away from me.
You believe love is only about you.
Every step I take, you want me to explain it first to you.
You need to understand, if you don't want to change,
Our love relationship will no longer grow.
Birds can't fly without wings, mouths can't talk without a tongue,
Love can't never grow by the power of someone else.
Baby, I know you get it and I get it, too.
Oil can give fat and butter can give fat, too.
This is not about boys and girls.
This is about our relationship needs to be on the right track,
But we make it seem like it is an impossible thing to do.
If we can learn how to dance from one step to two steps,
We shouldn't make life relationships so difficult.
One last thing, sweetheart, love grows and makes fruit,
But the seeds will never grow in just any place.
Love isn't luck and chance, it's a gift.

When you feel you need someone to talk to or
You need someone to keep you company,
You can call me, sweetheart.
When you feel you need someone to talk or
You need someone to keep you company,
You can call me, sweetheart.

You said you know me better than I know myself.

Our love relationship should be on the top of the world.
We would never tire of each other.
Life is a test; you must work hard and do things right.
You grade yourself for it. That's how life works.
The makers gained and the users lost.
When you use your imagination the right way,
Your dreams can come true to bless you and others.
Good love doesn't just fall on any relationship.
Relationships take hard work to build and grow good love.
When you see something clearly, you can describe it accurately,
But when you describe things you can't see, you sound like a fool.
This is one of the reasons love doesn't have a true meaning.
We can only describe it by the way we feel.
Baby, all I want you to understand you are right where you need to be.
You should not make a sound. You just need to trust and believe in me.
I will shower you with the honey of love to keep you blessed.
We can make ourselves be anything.
I love you and I wish you loved me, too.

When you feel you need someone to talk to or
You need someone to keep you company.
You can call me, sweetheart

When you feel you need someone to talk to or
You need someone to keep you company,
You can call me.

#17 – Meaning of Family

I love all the families around the world.
I believe we should love them all.
Then, our world can be better.

I know men who are considered helping angels in other family's lives.
However, their families have to ask others to help them.
There are relationships I've seen that would make me want to stay single.
We need to remember our children are watching what we are doing.
They are going to base their future relationships on how we handle ours.
We should always put our families first in everything we do.
A good listener learns more than a good talker.
We already know life isn't about us.
We still do things without thinking about who will be affected.
By the time we opened our eyes, it affects us more than anyone else.
Love is something we share, not give.
We can never love something and expect them to love us back.
But a little appreciation is more than a billion-dollar trophy.
We know we can make life great for us and our families if we aren't selfish.
Even if we don't have much, we can still live like kings and queens.

Life's menu is just like any other menu.
Everyone knows you can't make an omelet without eggs.
In the same way, a good family cannot grow without love.
Love is the first ingredient on a family recipe. Love is
the answer.

My family deserves my first love.
My family will give me the credit on my life's report card.
I don't want to fail when it comes to my family
relationship.
Love is the answer.

Let us do our best to make our families feel
They are the most important and valuable thing in
our lives.
They should have our attention every second of our life.
We need to remember our kids didn't ask us to give
them life.
We need to take great care of them,
Until they are ready to take care of themselves.
Our job is to make life explainable to them.
That means we need to do things with the proper life rules.
When we learn to love our family as God intended,
We will make things run smoothly for everyone around us.
We know we can't want what we don't want to give.
Life turns around the right direction when you
turn it right.
We should never want to make the same mistakes our
grandparents did.
We should just learn from them.
Today, our families need us more than ever.

We should never let them fall because of our negligence.
The stronger the foundation the longer it will take
to break it.
This is not rocket science, just simple things we all
should know.
We keep running after things that cannot love us.
We reject those who do, never realizing we are the
lucky ones.
They cry and we laugh. They are in pain and we celebrate.
Then, we wonder why things backfire on us.
This is why dogs say they are happy men don't know
What they are saying when they bark.
Love is the answer. With love, everything can be possible.

My family deserves my first love.
My family will give me the credit on my life's report card.
I don't want to fail when it comes to my family
relationship.
Love is the answer.

Two fingers are better than one, and three fingers are
better than two,
Sometimes, though, we have too many fingers on our lives!
We need to understand it isn't about the number of fingers,
It is what they do in your lives.
Do we really know the meaning of family?
If we did, our families would have our love, support,
appreciation and respect, joy, happiness, and peace.
We would never regret seeing another day.
Our world would be a pre-heaven place to live.

When you find love, take your time, and build a good foundation.

Be wise in everything you do especially with loving your family.
A family that can't be described by love is not a family.
If you don't want to finish it Please don't start it.
When you start a family, you must finish it to see the beauty of it.
Love is only the answer. You have it, you grow it by taking great care of it,
Then wait to see what it will turn out to be. Love is the answer.

My family deserves my first love.
My family will give me the credit on my life's report card.
I don't want to fail when it comes to my family relationship.
Love is the answer.

#18 – The Perfect Match

I didn't believe I could fall in love so quickly.
You are the perfect match for me.
You have everything I ever wanted.
Please, baby, tell me you are the one my life will end with.

(Man sings…)
When I look at myself in the mirror. All I can see is the reflection of you.

Your spirit manifests through my mind and controls my heart.
You are my beautiful flower, my angel, and every favorite thing in my life.
I can watch your pretty face and never get bored.
When I look at you, there are three things I can think of, Joy, happiness, and peace. I want you to know the way I feel.
Sometimes, I ask myself if you weren't here what I would do?
You are so perfect for me, I don't have a thing I would want to change.
We can walk slowly and get to know each other.
I haven't known you for too long,
But I already trust you with all the love I have.
I want you to understand nothing is impossible in life.
Talk to me and tell me how you feel.
Do you love me?
I'm willing to love you the way I should and never ever hurt you.

I didn't believe I can fall in love so quickly.
You are the perfect match for me.
You have everything I ever wanted.
Please, baby, tell me you are the one my life will end with.

(Woman sings…)
Listen, sweetheart, I hope you don't take it wrong.
I already had a few boyfriends before you came into the picture.
This is one of the reasons I want to take things slow.

The Reality of Life

You are an amazing person to be around.
Buy I don't want to go too fast.
I don't want to repeat the same mistake over and over.
I hope you understand and follow the rules of love.
I'm a complete girl who comes with the whole package.
I can cook delicious and healthy food like you have never tasted before.
All we need to start with is a new seed in our garden of love.
Let us make sure we take care of it and watch it grow, just like a newborn baby.
I can see you are my type and we will be fine together.
I'm ready to find out everything you like to make us happier every step we take. We can use love just like a jawbreaker. We can lick it, but never crush it.
My goal is to make you the happiest man alive.

I didn't believe I can fall in love so quickly.
You are the perfect match for me.
You have everything I ever wanted.
Please, baby, tell me you are the one my life will end with.

(Man sings…)
Listen, my sunflower,
I truly understand you so well.
Whatever way you play, the rules will be followed.
I don't want to make any mistakes when it comes to your rules.
Baby, trust me and I will trust you. Love is our way to live our life.
Whatever happens our love will be stronger and stronger.

I never thought girls like you still existed.
Let us put our love in a safety box where others don't have to be jealous of it.
We already know those who show off their love don't last long.
We just need to keep it real and simple.
We can do things privately, especially our vacation time.
We can learn the truth about each other.
Our fun times can be unlimited, you know what I mean.
We can learn to eat coco right out of the tree.
The thing we should do is promise each other…
If we find some bumps in our way, we won't let them make us fall.
We need to keep moving with a positive faith and never let it fade away.
Right now, my goal is for you to let me take great care of you

I didn't believe I can fall in love so quickly.
You are the perfect match for me.
You have everything I ever wanted.
Please, baby, tell me you are the one my life will end with.

#19–Father's Day

Father's Day arrives and I'm not ready.
The only thing I have ready is a piece of love.
I wish you appreciated it.

Dad, you know you mean the world to me.
I know there are millions of types of fathers.

But you don't have to worry about any other name,
but a loving, kind, superhero dad.
I know many people don't see your presence as a
kid's creator.
But I'm happy the way you have been doing things
in my life.
There is no way for me to call you anything better than a
loving dad.
It is not easy to find a real father who would care and
be ready to give his life to save his kids, but you did.
Your name becomes a lifetime tattoo
that can never erase from my heart.
I just want you to know you can turn into all skin
and bones.
I will always love you and never be ashamed of you.

Father's Day arrives and I'm not ready.
The only thing I have ready is a piece of love.
I wish you appreciated it.

I know when I see a good quality of thing.
You, Dad are the most quality dad I ever lay my eyes on.
Your promise was real and true,
Your yes didn't have any other meaning but yes.
Your love was the best quality of love.
I remember when you used to sing the song for me.
That song was recorded in my mind.
I have never heard anyone who can sing it better than you.
I want you to understand that,
I'm not telling you things to make you feel special.
You are the hero of my life.

No one can replace you or take your spot in my heart.
Happy Father's Day my one a million dad.

Father's Day arrives and I'm not ready.
The only thing I have ready is a piece of love.
I wish you appreciated it.

When it comes to taking great care of me,
It didn't matter how hot or cold the weather was,
You made sure it was the temperature I could handle.
No task was too hard for you to do
When it came to taking great care of me.
I don't know if all fathers deserve the prize you deserve.
If there is a better thing prize than a trophy,
Your name should be right in front where everyone
can see it.
You are my dad and you deserve the trophy of my life.
It doesn't matter what I give you, it will never be enough.
Happy Father's Day my lovely dad,
I wish there were more loving dads like you.
Happy Father's Day, dad. Enjoy.

Father's Day arrives and I'm not ready.
The only thing I have ready is a piece of love.
I wish you appreciated it.

God Songs

#20 – God's Army

I have God's army everywhere I go.
I have God's army everywhere I step.
Now I don't worry about anything anymore.
I have enough power to defeat my enemies.

Who are part of God's army?
All the servants of God
repeat that again.
Who are part of God's army?

God's army is:
Our Father who art in heaven.
Holy Spirit, to breathe into me,
that my thoughts may all be holy.
The Lord is my shepherd; I shall not want.
O gracious and holy Father,
gives us wisdom to perceive Him.
Now, Thank God's army for keeping you safe through
the night,
and watching over you during the day.

I have God's army everywhere I go.
I have God's army everywhere I step.
Now I don't worry about anything anymore.
I have enough power to defeat my enemies.

All the servants of God,
If you believe you have God's army with you.
Please tell me,
Who is part of God's Army?

God's Army is:
Christ with me, Christ before me,
Christ behind me, Christ in me.
God grants me the serenity
to accept the things I cannot change.
I will worship Thee, from the rising of the sun,
unto the going down of the same.
Lord, make me an instrument of Your peace.
I will lift up my eyes unto the hills.
From whence cometh my help.

I have God's army everywhere I go.
I have God's army everywhere I step.
Now I don't worry about anything anymore.
I have enough power to defeat my enemies.

All the servants of God,
If you believe you have God's army with you.
Please tell me,
Who is part of God's Army?

God's Army is:

The Soul of Christ sanctifies me,
The Body of Christ heals me.
May there always be work my hands to do.
May the strength of God pilot me, and
The power of God preserve me today.
I do not ask to walk smooth paths
Nor bear an easy load.
O Holy Spirit, descend plentifully into my heart.
Enlighten the dark corners of this neglected dwelling
and scatter Your cheerful beams.

No other armies can defeat Your powerful armies.
I better join this powerful team before it is too late.

I have God's army everywhere I go.
I have God's army everywhere I step.
Now I don't worry about anything anymore.
I have enough power to defeat my enemies.

One more time.

I have God's army everywhere I go.
I have God's army everywhere I step.
Now I don't worry about anything anymore.
I have enough power to defeat my enemies.

Amen, Amen, Amen.

#21 – Why Hasn't God Answered My Prayers?

Oh Lord, now I can understand why
You haven't answered my prayers.
Oh Lord, now I can see why
I have not received Your blessing.
Oh Lord, now I can understand why
My enemies will not leave me alone.

The truth will always be true
The false will always be false.
Our Father God is real and true
even though you don't want to believe it.
Our Father is powerful and faithful to all of us
When we believe in Him and do what He asks us to do.

Prayers are answered with time, effort, and
Hearts open to breaking free from our problems.
When we want the blessing of God to manifest,
We need to learn how God's prayers manifest first.
Prayers are the GPS to lead us to God's destination.

We don't need to work hard to find it.
We just need to follow God's rules the right way.
Be wise and be smart.
God's blessings are the way to
Breakthrough in your life.

Oh Lord, now I can understand why
You haven't answered my prayers.
Oh Lord, now I can see why

I have not received Your blessing.
Oh Lord, now I can understand why
My enemies will not leave me alone.

We all are smart in our own ways.
The ones who are really smart are
the ones who choose to do things right.
We should be thankful to God for
The power He gave us to rule the world.
We need to understand we are not God, though.
God is true, real, and understanding,
He is patient, powerful, and amazing.
The direction of God comes when we serve first.

We don't need to work hard to find it.
We just need to follow God's rules the right way.
Be wise and be smart.
God's blessings are the way to
Breakthrough in your life.

Oh Lord, now I can understand why
You haven't answered my prayers.
Oh Lord, now I can see why
I have not received Your blessing.
Oh Lord, now I can understand why
My enemies will not leave me alone.

Oh Lord, I know You are real.
However, You are not in my life to do everything for me.
You gave me all I ever needed
Including a brain to know right from wrong.

If I choose to do wrong, I should pay the consequences.
Life is the easiest when I do what is right.
God knows all of us. We are all God creatures.
But to call ourself a child of God, we must believe in God.
We must worship God the way He asks us to do.
If we do it wrong, we lack knowledge and understanding.

We don't need to work hard to find it.
We just need to follow God's rules the right way.
Be wise and be smart.
God's blessings are the way to
Breakthrough in your life.

Oh Lord, now I can understand why
You haven't answered my prayers.
Oh Lord, now I can see why
I have not received Your blessing.
Oh Lord, now I can understand why
My enemies will not leave me alone.

#22 – I Am Blessed

I'm blessed to have God in my life.
I'm blessed to have this beautiful life.
I'm blessed to I know I'm blessed.
Oh Lord, many people believe You need to give them
The world for them to know they are blessed.
I just want You to know I am satisfied
With the blessings I have received.

God has blessed us with life.

It is the most important blessing we have received.
We know we need God in our lives,
But do we know the Lord's policy for blessings?
We believe since we have God in our lives,
We should just leave everything to Him and
He will take great care of it all.
Our Lord is faithful, powerful, and helpful.
He will help us with what we can't do.
I just want to thank You, God for
The knowledge and understanding to know
Your policy for blessing my life.

I'm blessed to have God in my life.
I'm blessed to have this beautiful life.
I'm blessed to I know I'm blessed.
Oh Lord, many people believe You need to give them
The world for them to know they are blessed.
I just want You to know I am satisfied
With the blessings I have received.

Oh Lord, why would I ask You
for a car, an airplane, and a house?
I know You gave us the knowledge and
Hands to build these things on our own.
Instead, I should ask You to keep us safe and
Bless us to be productive in everything we touch.
I should ask You to keep Your eyes on
Me and my family every step we make.
Oh Lord, I know You are here to help us.
But I never want to use You as my slave.
If You wanted to do everything for us,

We wouldn't have the hands, legs, and eyes
To see how beautiful life can be.
You have one person who believes in You.
I have You in my life and
You will be my Lord until I die.

I'm blessed to have God in my life.
I'm blessed to have this beautiful life.
I'm blessed to I know I'm blessed.
Oh Lord, many people believe You need to give them
The world for them to know they are blessed.
I just want You to know I am satisfied
With the blessings I have received.

I accepted You, believed in You, I worshiped You,
Then I received my blessing from You.
Who else could make me so unique than You?
You are my Lord and I will always be grateful.
No matter how bad the weather is
You have never missed my phone call.
Even when I am not able to call You,
You are always with me when I need You.
What a beautiful God I have.
What a wonderful God I have.
What a powerful God I have.
I will always be true to You until I die.

I'm blessed to have God in my life.
I'm blessed to have this beautiful life.
I'm blessed to I know I'm blessed.
Oh Lord, many people believe You need to give them

The world for them to know they are blessed.
I just want You to know I am satisfied
With the blessings I have received.

#23 – God Please Give Me a Sign

God, please give me a sign.
When my enemies are going to attack me.
God, please give me a sign.
When others have lied to me.
God, please give me a sign,
When others want to corrupt my mind.
Even though we need to trust one another,
We can't really know who to trust.
So, Your sign will protect me from doing
Things that are wrong, but I think are right.

We should have discernment to understand,
When others are in need of help.
Christian people should be all for one and one for all.
Hold my hand and I will hold your hand.
If I can make it to eternal life,
There is no reason for you to miss it.
Christians should never wish others anything bad
We should always show them God's love
Even though they are our worst enemies.

God, please give me a sign.
When my enemies are going to attack me.
God, please give me a sign.
When others have lied to me.

God, please give me a sign,
When others want to corrupt my mind.
Even though we need to trust one another,
We can't really know who to trust.
So, Your sign will protect me from doing
Things that are wrong, but I think are right.

We always want good quality things in our lives.
God's will always bring us
The best quality things we need.
If we don't want to work harder to do our part,
It will be harder to receive the harvest you work for.
God promised us He will always be with us,
But we need to know how to be with Him, too.
God's words will do what it takes to
Save us from an attack against our lives.
All we need to do is to ask and
The Lord will give you a sign.

God, please give me a sign.
When my enemies are going to attack me.
God, please give me a sign.
When others have lied to me.
God, please give me a sign,
When others want to corrupt my mind.
Even though we need to trust one another,
We can't really know who to trust.
So, Your sign will protect me from doing
Things that are wrong, but I think are right.

#24 – What Would I Do If…?

What would I do if,
I didn't have God in my life?
What would I do if,
I didn't know how to follow God's rules?
What would I do if,
I didn't give my life to God?

My life would be a total loss.
My life would be like a car without breaks.
My life would be like a robot without a soul.

These are the things that make me happy.
These are the things that make me blessed,
Every single day in my life.
These are the things that make me,
Beautiful in every moment.
What makes you happy, blessed, and beautiful?

I have so many rewards from You, my Lord.
What are these rewards?
The rewards are love, joy, and peace.
The trophies are patience and faithfulness.
The gifts are royalty and self-control.
Medals are forgiveness and goodness.

Here are all the things I did to receive
these rewards from the Lord today.
I believe in God the way He asked me to.
I follow His rules the way He told me.

I read a verse, a psalm, and pray three times a day.

I remember when I was young,
I believed having God in my life was hard to do.
When I got older, I read the Bible the right way and understood the goodness of God.
Even though I had a lot of negativities in my life,
I tried my best to overcome them,
without creating any enemies.
I transformed into someone,
I never thought I could become.
It doesn't matter what anyone says,
You are true, amazing, wonderful, and powerful.
I am thankful You are my God.

Please sing this song One more time.

#25 – Your Name Is Beautiful

What is a beautiful name? God.
What is a beautiful name? The Lord.
What is a beautiful name? Jesus Christ.
Now I can see why my name is beautiful.

The workers represent the company.
When the workers fail to follow the company rules,
They destroy the company's reputation.
We are human beings, and we represent You.

I will be true to You even if it costs my life.
I will always tell the truth,

Even though they don't like me for it.
I will live a life of truth, God's truth.
There is nothing better than being true to You.

What is a beautiful name? God.
What is a beautiful name? The Lord.
What is a beautiful name? Jesus Christ.
Now I can see why my name is beautiful.

Life is good. Everything happens for a reason.
The Lord gives us life for free,
It is the most important and expensive thing on earth.
Our Father God doesn't make mistakes, but we do.
We know the best way is to live the life of truth.
Listen to your heart and see how important
It is to live the life of truth, God's truth.

I will be true to You even if it costs my life.
I will always tell the truth,
Even though they don't like me for it.
I will live a life of truth, God's truth.
There is nothing better than being true to You.

What is a beautiful name? God.
What is a beautiful name? The Lord.
What is a beautiful name? Jesus Christ.
Now I can see why my name is beautiful.

I know Your name is beautiful and powerful.
Your name will always be beautiful and powerful.
How can we make the name of Christians

Beautiful and powerful, too?
We have your DNA for You are our father.
We should appreciate, respect, love, and praise You.
We need to give our brothers and sisters
The same treatment we have been given by You.
You didn't create us to be evil to each other.
Help us to understand we are brothers and sisters
Who should love each other to the end of our lives.

What is a beautiful name? God.
What is a beautiful name? The Lord.
What is a beautiful name? Jesus Christ.
Now I can see why my name is beautiful.

#26 – I Promised Myself

I promise myself to follow Your Word
The way You tell me to, my God.
I promise myself to follow your rules,
The way You instructed me to, my Lord.
I promised myself to worship You the right way.
I promised myself to do things right and
Love everyone including my enemies.
Please Lord, give me strength to
Keep my promises until the last breath of my life.

The first thing You gave me is life.
I really appreciate the fact You choose me.
You gave me life to enjoy until it is time.
To go to eternity to enjoy our life there with You.
You gave us free will to make our own choices.

I promise myself to use my will to
only do things that are right even though I'm not perfect,
I will always be ready to repair my mistakes and
Continue my life more carefully than before.
No one can have a perfect life and ready
So, we need to feed ourselves God's Word.

I also promise myself to respect myself.
Others including animals and trees.
I promise myself to help those who need help.
I promise myself to do things by Your rules of life.
Please Lord, give me strength to keep my promises
Until the last breath of my life.

The Word of God are easy to understand and
Easy to follow when you promise yourself to obey them.
We should believe God's Word and follow the rules of life.
It is the only way to achieve world peace.
We need to believe in God, trust God, and
Follow the rules of God the right way.
Then we will see the miracles God will work.

There are a few more promises I made to myself.
I promise myself to tell the truth all the time.
I promise myself to live life to the fullest.
I promise myself never to intentionally hurt anyone.
I promise myself to treat everyone the same
Even though they choose to be my worst enemies.
Please Lord, give me strength to
keep my promises until the last breath of my life.

Brothers and sisters, the Words of God are for everyone.
who loves the truth and wishes to live the truth of life.
God's Word should be the reflected in our lives and
Everything we do since we are the children of God.
Yes, we make mistakes, but our Father forgives us.
When we try to correct them and do better.
Sometimes things happen in our lives,
But we can learn from our mistakes.
We can find the goodness of ourselves to
make the best way of life for everyone around us.

I promise myself to follow Your Word
The way You tell me to, my God.
I promise myself to follow your rules,
The way You instructed me to, my Lord.
I promised myself to worship You the right way.
I promised myself to do things right and
Love everyone including my enemies.
Please Lord, give me strength to
Keep my promises until the last breath of my life.

#27–My Life Became a Diamond

What's an easy way to get the ticket going to heaven?
Life has its own rules even though,
We don't want to believe it.
Our soul is a bank account for our life.
If we don't know how to feed it,
We can have a broken soul while here.
I didn't know how to load
My soul with the blessing of God.

I tried to ask questions, but no one could answer me.
When I started reading the Bible,
I found a way to fulfill my destiny.
God's way, the right way.

I used to cry and asked God not to see another day.
I used to feed the devil's way to my soul without
knowing it.
When I paused to find a way to get closer to God,
That day was a breakthrough in my life.
My life became a diamond I found for the first time.
Lord, You showed me the way to get to You.
There was no way for me to miss it.

Now, doing good will be my everyday thing.
Praying for my enemies to change to be good,
Giving, helping, and treating others the right way
Will be my breakfast every day.
Oh Lord, now I know what You really need from me.

We should never underestimate our Father God.
He knows what we need and when we need it.
He knows what He is going to do to lead us to it.
He created each creature to help, protect, and
Be there when we need each other.
Our Father God had the world planned,
Before He began creating it.
He knows we can never be loved alone.
I know we should love ourselves first,
But if we can't share our love with others,
Then our love will not make any sense.

Love makes us want to share and
That is what makes love grow.

Now, doing good will be my everyday thing.
Praying for my enemies to change to be good,
Giving, helping, and treating others the right way
Will be my breakfast every day.
Oh Lord, now I know what You really need from me.

#28 – The Power of Prayers

A Friday night when I was praying,
I closed my eyes to apply a deeper prayer,
It felt like I saw a shooting star and,
I heard someone tell me to make a wish.

I wish I could make everyone know
How powerful You are, my God.
I wish I could make everyone
Understand how beautiful life can be.
I wish I could have a world peace where
We can love each other in the eyes of God.

I wish my Lord could extend
The life of those who never had a chance
To know how beautiful life can be.
I wish our leadership would drop the money and
Pick up the Bible to teach us how
We can be better Christians.

Sometimes, I wish to pray out loud.

Sometimes, I wish to pray softly.
Sometimes, I wish to pray with a harmony
In my heart to feel the direction I'm going.

When you have God in your life, you never be alone.
Our Father is never tired of hearing from us,
Even though sometimes we choose to make a U-turn.
There are a few ways you can feel the power of prayers.
Prayers sometimes work by emotion.
Use the power of emotional prayers and
You will see how easy all your homework will get done.
You will see how miracles are connected and
Bring the blessing of light into your life.

It's not difficult to understand the power of prayers.
If we would pray for each other, and
See the beauty of each other.
If we could understand when and how to
Use our prayer power to defeat our enemies.
We have a lot of things we can do if we choose,
To believe in God and worship God the right way.
We have unlimited power through our prayers.
It will get stronger and stronger when you use it.

Today, all I really wish is for us to work together and
Use the power of prayer our Father God has
Given us to make release miracles in others' lives.
Let us use the power of prayer to cure others for free.
Then they can see why we believe in God and
Why we represent our Father in everything we do.
Our Father will thank us when we do.

I wish I could share my life with the
One who has difficulty with theirs.
I wish I could give everyone a chance
to see and feel the beauty of life.
I wish I was an angel to watch over
The ones who can see for themselves.

I know we live in a world of sadness and happiness.
I know we live in ugliness and beauty.
Oh Lord, my wish is for Christians to be united.
Every Christian needs to see and talk about
What we believe about You, my Lord.
When we follow You the right way, my God,
We should see miracles and be powerful prayers.
I truly believe, if we use our prayer power to pray
Your miracles on each other in the name of Jesus,
All our lives would be set free from the devil.

I wish I could make everyone know,
How powerful You are, my God.
I wish I could make everyone
Understand how beautiful life can be.
I wish I could have a world peace where
We can love each other in the eyes of God.

#29 – Christmas

It shouldn't matter how Christmas enters your house,
As long as you see Christmas day as Jesus' birthday.
You should always celebrate it with your whole heart.

When you look at Christmas holidays.
All you can see is growing love between us.
Even though we don't have anything to celebrate with,
just hearing the name of Christmas go along with
the Christmas tree should bring joy and happiness in
our hearts.

Christmas is for everyone to celebrate Jesus' birthday.
We should use Christmas day to thank the Lord
For His great gift to us.
The whole month of December is
Called the Christmas season.
There are Christmas songs on every radio station.
Birds sing earlier in the morning,
The flowers look more beautiful and,
Everywhere smells like cinnamon gingerbread.
I know there are a lot of holidays in the year,
But no holiday can compare with Christmas.
Because Christmas is for everyone,
That is the beauty of Christmas,
That is the beauty of Christmas.

When you look at Christmas holidays.
All you can see is growing love between us.
Even though we don't have anything to celebrate with,
just hearing the name of Christmas go along with
the Christmas tree should bring joy and happiness in
our hearts.

The Christmas tree should bring joy and
Happiness in our hearts.

Christmas brings pure love between all of us.
Christmas day starts and ends with smiles.
All the kids around the world
Wish Christmas could be every day.
Christmas is the only holiday
Kisses, handshakes, and hugging feel so good.
Food tastes so good, we are ready weeks before Christmas.
Christmas is not just a holiday.
It is love, respect, joy, peace, and sharing.
That is the beauty of Christmas,
That is the beauty of Christmas.

When you look at Christmas holidays.
All you can see is growing love between us.
Even though we don't have anything to celebrate with,
just hearing the name of Christmas go along with
the Christmas tree should bring joy and happiness in
our hearts.

I remembered when I was a child, though I didn't have
any gifts,
The joy I had was worth more than any gift.
Christmas joy is very special.
Christmas joy is real.
Christmas love is pure and unique.
Celebrating Christmas means celebrating
Love, respect, appreciation, peace, and happiness.

Ho ho, ho, ho, Christmas day is arriving.
Ho, ho, ho, ho, you don't need anything to celebrate
Christmas.

Ho, ho, ho, ho all you really need to celebrate Christmas
Is to be alive, healthy, and see the joy in my family.
Merry Christmas to you and everyone around the world.

All I need to celebrate Christmas is for me to be healthy.
All I need to celebrate Christmas is a little piece of love.
All I need to celebrate Christmas is
seeing the joy in my family.

Baby I know this year brings us so many difficulties to
make us not celebrate Christmas the way we should.
But we will use this energy to boost our Christmas holidays to be the best day we ever had.
Baby, you will be my Christmas tree, your eyes will be the
stars light to shine in me and your lips will be the wire to
connect the Christmas love between us.
Baby, this Christmas holiday.
There isn't anything we will not do to make Christmas
bell rings louder than before and wish for our love to
last forever.
Because, my Christmas will start with you and end up with
you by looking at your happiness, joy in your life.
Merry Christmas to you and everyone around the world.

All I need to celebrate Christmas is for me to be healthy.
All I need to celebrate Christmas is a little piece of love.
All I need to celebrate Christmas is
seeing the joy in my family.

Baby, everytime I remember Christmas is the day
Christ was born.

I can see Christmas day is a day to celebrate you too, and wish for our love to continue growing, and blessed the name of the lord.
Christmas is a day when the rain of love falls harder, and the sun shines the rainbow of love all over the world without thinking of whether you are rich or poor.
Baby, the world can take Christmas out of me.
But, they can't take me out of Christmas.
Everytime I see Christmas day.
It reflects on you.
Because, we use the love, respect, peace, joy and happiness of Christmas to celebrate the rest of the year.
This is one of the reasons why our bucket list of love is blessed all year, even though we don't have anything. I wish you Merry Christmas, and everyone around the world.

All I need to celebrate Christmas is for me to be healthy.
All I need to celebrate Christmas is a little piece of love.
All I need to celebrate Christmas is
seeing the joy in my family.

Christmas has a unique smell.
Christmas brings love with a unique flavor.
Christmas love is pure and unique for all.
Christmas plants trees of love in our hearts.
Christmas brings treats, no trick to show how important Christmas love is in our lives.
Merry Christmas to you and everyone around the world.

All I need to celebrate Christmas is for me to be healthy.
All I need to celebrate Christmas is a little piece of love.

All I need to celebrate Christmas is
seeing the joy in my family.

#30 – You Can Fly Higher Than an Eagle

I believe you can do it
I believe you can make it
If you work harder and never give up.
There is no way for you not to make it
You can finish if you have confidence in yourself.

I don't know who you really are, but you do.
I don't know how far you can go, but you know.
You know you have today,
But you don't know about tomorrow.
You know how important your
Gift and your talents mean to you.
Failure happens to the one who stops trying.
You can feel nervous and scared and
Wish you could quit before you start your game.
I was in your shoes once in my life.
When I remembered how beautiful life can be
I took two steps back to refresh my memory.
It took me to the time when I was a child and,
My parents used to tell me to keep my balance and
my faith and no obstacles will be too hard for me to
Hit the buzzer without one false step.
They used to say life is just like iron.
You can melt it down and see how many beautiful
Things you can make to use every drop of it.
A single hit can make your dreams come true.

The Reality of Life

One kick can make a touchdown.
A single throw can make the three winning goal points.
Your battles start and end with you.
It takes common sense to be a genius.
A real genius is the one who knows how to
Turn their talents into a trophy without
Thinking of the roots they came from.

You can fly higher than an eagle if you believe you can.
You can run faster than a rocket if you believe you can.
Life isn't about what people think you can or can't do.
You are the only one who knows the limits of your goals.

Life is like a rainbow, but that doesn't mean
All the colors will fit you.
Everyone wants the taste of winning better than losing,
But the only way you get the real taste out of winning is
When you know the taste of losing.
Every bird flies, but they don't flap their wings the same way. You are special and unique in every movement you make.
Use your hands, your feet, or any part of your body
To be the hero of your life. It doesn't take much,
Just a little hard work with a little confidence.
Self-control can make you stand strong.
Strength can make you believe in yourself and
Give you power to reach the last piece of the energy
You need to win your victory.
Your technique will show the world who you really are
Without explaining a thing about yourself.

Talent can play magic rules, but the only one who knows it is
The one who can find their talent themselves.
Find your talent, use it well, and let it take you
To the last competition of your game.
You can do it, you can make it.
All it takes is a little bit of hard work
With confidence in yourself.

You can fly higher than an eagle if you believe you can.
You can run faster than a rocket if you believe you can.
Life isn't about what people think you can or can't do.
You are the only one who knows the limits of your goals.

The only time you are a loser in your game is
When you know you didn't do your best.
As long as you do your best,
It doesn't matter how bad you lose.
You always need to consider yourself a winner.

The only time you can receive your blessing is
when you know what you wish for.
Hit it, catch it, kick it, and throw it the hardest you can.
The game is not over yet. The victory can be yours.
You should never leave without it.
Be ready to manifest the winner you always want to celebrate. Clapping, jumping, and blowing your whistle.
You can lean to the right, lean to the left,
You can rise up and shake your body to celebrate victory.
You can do it and you can make it if you want to.
All it takes is a little hard work.

Don't wait in line to enjoy your own victory.

I know for sure you can do it, you can make it.
All it takes is a little bit of hard work
And confidence in yourself.

You can fly higher than an eagle if you believe you can.
You can run faster than a rocket if you believe you can.
Life isn't about what people think you can or can't do.
You are the only one who knows the limits of your goals.

#31 – I'm Proud to be an American

I'm American and I'm proud to be American.
This is one of the reasons I try to know my rights.
Americans should know our rights, but many don't.
We should be the ones who represent our country, but we don't. America is the best country in the world, but we don't know it Most of us don't know what the fifty stars
And the thirteen stripes represent.
What are our rights? What are the rules of law?
Why do we need to vote?
What are the cabinet-level positions?
What does the judicial branch do?
How old do we need to be president in our country?
What are the reasons colonists came to our country?
Who is our current president?
Who were Abraham Lincoln and JFK?

I'm American, I would be ashamed if I didn't know
What makes my country beautiful.

I'm American, I would be ashamed if I didn't know
What makes my country beautiful.

Why are we the greatest people on earth?
Who lived in America before the Europeans arrived?
Why did the colonists fight the British?
What group of people were taken to America and sold as slaves? Who wrote the Declaration of Independence?
Why was Benjamin Franklin famous?
Who was the father of our country?

I'm American, I would be ashamed if I didn't know
What makes my country beautiful.
I'm American, I would be ashamed if I didn't know
What makes my country beautiful.

We say we are united, so why don't we love, respect,
Support each other, appreciate we are Americans and
Work together for the benefit of our country?
Why don't we spend more money on our kids' education?
Why do we have so many homeless people on the streets?
Why don't we do something to reduce poverty in America?

I'm American, I would be ashamed if I didn't know
What makes my country beautiful.
I'm American, I would be ashamed if I didn't know
What makes my country beautiful.

Our country should have one united direction.
We should help each other in everything we do.
Who are our worst enemies?

The Reality of Life

Why do we celebrate July 4?
Who is Martin Luther King?
Who was the first black president?

My name is America, the greatest country in the world.
My name is America, the strongest and
richest country in the world.
Everyone loves my democracy and my law.
I'm America, I am always ready to help everyone
Who needs help even though I know they hate me.
Everyone wants to come to America and be fed,
But never appreciate America for the goodness of love.
I'm America, the most powerful country in the world.
I don't let loud noises make me lose control.

You need to know what the symbols of America represent:
The Bald Eagle means I can fly higher and see miles away.
I have an amazing way of hunting and
When I grab on something, I don't let go until I
see the end.

The Liberty Bell means, when I drop,
it will turn your world upside down.
The Statue Of Liberty means I have God with me.
Mount Rushmore means before you think of challenging
America, you need to know how good your shovel can dig.
The flag of the United States stands for strength in
adversity.
The American Bison means you must be crazy
If you want to go head-to-head with me.
You better think a million times

before you think of messing with me.

I'm American, I would be ashamed if I didn't know
What makes my country beautiful.
I'm American, I would be ashamed if I didn't know
What makes my country beautiful.

www.ingramcontent.com/pod-product-compliance
Ingram Content Group UK Ltd.
Pitfield, Milton Keynes, MK11 3LW, UK
UKHW041949230426
12048UKWH00008B/237

9 781662 882777